marijuana cooking

good medicine made easy

marijuana cooking

good medicine made easy

Bliss Cameron
and Veronica Greene

Green Candy Press

Marijuana Cooking: Good Medicine Made Easy
by Bliss Cameron and Veronica Greene

ISBN 1-931160-32-5
Published by Green Candy Press
www.greencandypress.com

Cover and interior photography: Pepper Design
Design: Ian Phillips

Printed in China
Massively Distributed by P.G.W.

Dedicated to all of the medical marijuana patients and individuals who continue to work for legal, safe and affordable access to this medicine.

Table of contents

Page 19

Page 21

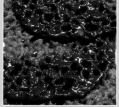

Page 31

Page 35

Page 47

Introduction

Bliss Cameron

I was actively involved with a community group working to legalize marijuana as medicine when Proposition 215 was passed by the people of the state of California in 1996. Patients were now able grow and use cannabis as medicine with an approval or recommendation from their doctors. As people became more aware that marijuana was medicine, questions arose regarding the need to regulate dosage and administer it in innovative ways.

One member of the group was a caregiver for his wife who had been using marijuana successfully to control the symptoms of glaucoma. They had found that ingesting cannabis was the most effective way to do this. This caregiver had, through trial and error, found a way to standardize the dose, which is critical for patients. Ingesting cannabis is very effective for many ailments, but it is imperative that the dose be standardized as too little is not effective, and too much can have side effects of its own. I'm a patient, too, and I wanted to learn how to do this for myself. By following the directions given by this caregiver, and through trial and error over the years, I've learned how to make baked goods that have been used successfully by many patients to control pain, increase appetite when needed, provide restful sleep and alleviate many symptoms from a wide range of medical conditions.

Coauthor Veronica Greene began making butter and cookies, using this method, with great success. She soon developed an extraction process for making cannabis/canola oil to meet special dietary needs of patients she was helping. We wrote this book to share these processes with patients and caregivers, using standard kitchen utensils and measurements. We are sharing what we've done that works for us. It can work for you, too.

1

A message for first time users

The initial response when smoking or ingesting marijuana varies from person to person. In addition to the desired medicinal effects, including a reduction of body pain, a lessening of inflammation, control over muscle spasms and positive shifts in emotional and mental states, marijuana can affect the body and mind in many ways. People use marijuana recreationally because of its ability to induce and magnify pleasurable sensations. Some of the common sensory experiences of being "high" can include a heightened attentiveness to touch, taste and sound and an increased interest in food and music.

There are some people, however, who find that marijuana makes them feel uncomfortable. This can be related to a person's temperament, physiology or mood. If, as is prevalent under the current "war against drugs," a person has been educated to believe that marijuana is harmful, it is particularly important to discuss this with a recommending doctor or other patients who have overcome these fears.

Other reported responses to marijuana use, perceived positively by some and negatively by others, include being in a dreamlike state, experiencing a disruption of concentration or short-term memory, becoming restless and talkative, seeing humor in everything, sensing that time has "expanded," and having altered judgment and coordination. These responses are more pronounced with larger doses, making it important for a novice to take only small amounts. It is a good idea to have an experienced person with you the first time you use marijuana. This person can talk you through any unexpected effects. The key is to just "chill out," knowing that this will all pass, without any permanent harm to the body or mind.

Keeping a journal can help you understand personal responses and needs. There are so many variables, including the potency and strain of the marijuana and your individual mind-set, which can alter the outcome. Some people will determine that marijuana is simply not their medicine. Others will find it life altering, offering a multiplicity of benefits.

Making marijuana butter and oil extracts

In this book we will show you four ways to extract the THC and other active cannabinoids from marijuana. The plant material is ultimately strained out in all four methods, resulting in butter or oil that is easily digested and may be used in standard recipes in the same way one would use regular butter and oil. These four methods are:

I: Ground marijuana in clarified butter
II. Ground marijuana in oil
III. Whole marijuana in water with butter
IV. Whole marijuana in water with coconut oil

All of these processes can be carried out using the following kitchen tools:

• a large pot (methods III & IV)
• bowls for cleaning/sorting the marijuana
• measuring cups
• cheesecloth (for methods III & IV)
• spoon or spatula for stirring
• a blender for grinding marijuana (for methods I & II)
• a scale to weigh the marijuana
• a Crock-Pot (for methods I & II)
• a strainer

Step 2

Step 1

Step 2

Method I: Ground Marijuana in Clarified Butter

Preparing the Cannabis

The ratio of cannabis to butter originally recommended to us was 2 ounces of cannabis for 3 pounds of butter. We have since been using a 1:1 ratio of 1 ounce of cannabis to 1 pound of butter, and find that this makes a good product. The form of cannabis varies, however. There's the bud, usually carefully trimmed and considered the highest source of THC and other cannabinoids (referred to as THC+). When using bud, the ratio can be from 1 ounce of cannabis to 2 pounds of butter or a bit higher, to 2 ounces of cannabis to 3 pounds of butter. There's the trim, which consists of small leaves cut from the buds. The basic ratio of 1 ounce of cannabis to 1 pound of butter is good for trim. There's leaf, which is taken from the plant at several stages of growth. A good ratio for leaf is 1½ to 2 ounces of cannabis to 1 pound butter as the THC+ content is lower in leaf than in trim. The potency will vary widely depending on which of these forms is used. I'm fortunate to have a regular supply of fairly consistently potent cannabis and choose to use bud trim as it has been more available than bud

and has a high THC+ content. It's important, however, to emphasize that the strain and maturity of the plant also play into the strength.

The first time you use a source of cannabis, we recommend that you test the end product by eating just one cookie or piece of cake and waiting at least 2 hours. Note the effect. It is helpful to keep a journal of the process, recording the strain of cannabis, the form (leaf, trim, bud or a mix), the ratio of cannabis to butter used, and the potency and effectiveness of the finished butter. You can take this journal to your recommending doctor to demonstrate the amount of cannabis you require.

Step 1: Clean the cannabis by removing large stems.

Step 2: Put the cleaned cannabis in a blender, food processor or coffee grinder and coarsely grind. When I initially tried this process, I bought a small coffee grinder and designated it just for this task, but soon I was making larger batches of butter so I switched to using a blender instead. Be careful not to overprocess. If the cannabis is too fine, it will be difficult to strain after cooking. Straining the finished butter will take out most of the leaf material. The cannabis plant has barbs on the ends of the leaf fronds, and these can easily upset a delicate stomach.

Clarifying the Butter

This is a simple process during which you heat up the butter several times to remove the excess moisture in it. I always put the Crock-Pot on low only, mostly because I have a tendency to forget about the pot and I know if I leave it on low it won't burn.

Step 1: Heat the butter until the side of the Crock-Pot feels uncomfortable to the touch of your full palm, then turn the Crock-Pot off. Skim off the foam that has risen to the top of the pot.

Step 2: Repeat this twice more, each time letting the butter cool fully before you reheat it. After skimming the third time, add the marijuana leaf.

Step 3: Stir. Bring to a simmer. Continue to simmer, stirring occasionally, for 1-2 hours.

Step 4: Cool for up to 8 hours. Then, in a new series of heatings and coolings, repeat heating, stirring and cooling down 2 more times. The increase in potency it produces is worth the investment in time. By the third heating, the butter will have a thicker consistency.

Step 5: Set a strainer with a relatively fine mesh on top of a large measuring bowl. The bowl will catch the strained butter.

Step 6: Slowly pour the butter into the strainer. Use a large serving spoon to press the remaining butter out of the leaf material. Squeeze out as much of the remaining butter as you can.

Step 7: Pour the butter into a measuring cup.

Step 8: Put the finished product in 1-cup containers, ready to use when needed. ✳

Step 3

Step 5

Step 6

Step 7

Step 8

Method II: Ground Marijuana in Oil

Step 1

Step 2

Step 3

Step 4

Step 5

This method is less time consuming and lower in fat than the butter method, but something is lost with regard to flavor when using the oil infusion as opposed to the butter infusion.

Step 1: Place 6 cups of canola oil in a Crock-Pot.

Step 2: You do *not* have to clarify it. Set the Crock-Pot on low and allow it to heat up until the Crock-Pot is too hot to press your hand against. Prepare the marijuana leaf as described in method I, (4 ounces), then pour it into the Crock-Pot and stir.

Step 3: Let sit for 3 days, reheating the mixture each day, and straining as in method I on the third day, as follows.

Step 4: Pour through a strainer into a large measuring bowl.

Step 5: Press the remaining oil out of the leaf material.

Step 6: Discard the leaf material. Here is how the finished oil looks:

You can keep the finished oil in a canning jar or any other suitable tightly sealed container in the refrigerator for up to 8 weeks. ✸

Method III: Whole Marijuana in Water with Butter

Step 1

Water Extraction

The following uses water with the marijuana and butter. Simmering the cannabis in water helps to break down the active ingredients. Because THC+ is only soluble in fat or alcohol, these active ingredients end up in the butter and the water can be discarded with no reduction in potency. This method also retains the cream in the butter as the butter is not clarified. This helps to produce a richer cookie, such as a shortbread, if that is important to the patient. It also eliminates the need to grind the marijuana. It does, however, require a larger pot and the need to refrigerate for an additional 24 hours. If time is a consideration, you may want to stick with method I.

Step I: Fill a large pot about half full with water. Add marijuana. This process does not require the careful cleaning or grinding needed in methods I and II. You can even use stems and whole leaves. I use 1 ounce of marijuana for one pound of butter. If the final product turns out to be too potent for you, reduce the amount of herb. Increase if a more potent medicine is needed.

Step 2: Bring to a boil, stirring once or twice. Reduce to a simmer and continue simmering for about 1 hour.

Step 2

Step 3: Add butter in proportion to amount of marijuana used. The butter does not need to be clarified. Slowly return to a simmer, stirring gently. Simmer for at least 1 hour. Remove from heat and allow to cool completely. Repeat the simmering/cooling process twice for the most potent butter. I usually do this over 2 days, covering the pot while it cools.

Step 3

Step 4: Now come the preparations for straining. Do this step right after the final simmering while the water is still hot. Use caution as the pot can be heavy. Find a second pot or bowl, at least as large as the first. Place a strainer or colander over the pot. Place a piece of cheesecloth over the strainer or colander. The cheesecloth can be eliminated, but I find it makes it easier to separate the herb from the water.

Step 4

Step 5

Step 6

Step 7

Step 8

Step 9

Step 5: Slowly pour the butter/water/herb mixture over the strainer. Allow to cool.

Step 6: When it is cool enough to handle, fold the cheesecloth around the herb and lift it out of the strainer.

Step 7: Twist the cheesecloth bundle and press with the back of a spoon. To recover the maximum amount of butter, pour 1-2 cups of boiling water over the herb while it rests in the strainer. Allow to cool enough to squeeze out this additional water. Discard the herb.

Step 8: Now we're ready to refrigerate. Pour liquid into a pot that will fit in your refrigerator. Cover, let cool, and then refrigerate this water/butter mixture for at least 24 hours. The butter will harden on top of the water.

Step 9: After the mixture has been refrigerated for 24 hours, it's time to separate the butter from the water. Cut a pie-shaped piece of butter and remove it from the water.

Step 10: Pull off remaining chunks of butter.

Step 11: To dry the butter, place the chunks of butter on a towel (paper towels will work) and gently pat excess water off of the bottom of the chunks.

Step 12: The surface of the butter that has been in contact with the water may be mushy. Gently scrape if desired. I save this mush to use in a recipe like the one for brownies, which will tolerate the addition of some water.

Step 13: You will now have several chunks of beautiful light green butter. Place them in a small pan and melt until you again have a liquid.

Step 14: For storage, pour liquid butter into measured containers: I use wide-mouth mason jars that contain one cup and recommend using containers that allow you to premeasure the butter according to your needs. Cover, cool, and refrigerate. If you do not plan to use the butter within the next week, freeze. Remove from refrigerator before using to soften. ✷

Step 10

Step 11

Step 12

Step 13

Step 14

Method IV: Whole Marijuana in Water with Coconut Oil

This method may be used for those who have dietary restrictions and do not want to use butter. Begin with a high-quality coconut oil. Because this oil is more expensive than butter, I usually make only 1 pound at a time, using a 1:1 ratio: 1 ounce of cannabis to a 14-ounce jar of coconut oil. This oil usually comes in 14-, not 16-ounce jars.

Step 1: Fill a small pot about half full with water. Add marijuana. Bring to a simmer, stirring occasionally, for up to an hour to break down the marijuana.

Step 2: Add the coconut oil. Stir gently and bring to a simmer. Remove from heat.

Step 3: Let sit at room temperature for up to 2 days. This slow extraction process will not break down the coconut oil.

Step 4: Reheat until oil is melted.

Step 5: Strain, refrigerate, and separate the oil from the water as shown in method III, steps 4–14. Coconut oil will harden like the butter but doesn't get the mush on the bottom. Note that coconut oil becomes white when it hardens, masking the green color of the herb, but rest assured, the potency is the same. The green color is restored when the oil is melted.

Summary

After following one of the four methods described above, you should now have a supply of premeasured containers of very fine marijuana butter or oil that you may use in any recipe that calls for butter or oil. ✱

When you can't wait
Quick ways to ingest cannabis butter or oil

Before we launch into recipes, it should be noted that sometimes a patient may urgently need to ingest some cannabis, but doesn't have the time or energy to bake. Here are some quick ways to put your cannabis butter or oil where it counts. Try the following:

Pot Corn
Melt cannabis butter and put on popcorn. Be careful about amounts, keeping in mind that more than 2 teaspoons is a very strong dose.

Bread 'n' Butter
Again, measure carefully. We would recommend one teaspoon for one slice of bread. If you're still hungry, eat more with regular butter!

Mother's Milk
I was reminded of a recipe that was a favorite of an elderly man who experienced a loss of appetite. He loved this Mother's Milk! Use 1 quart of whole milk, rice milk or soy milk and $1/4$ to $1/2$ ounce of cannabis leaf or trim. Soak cannabis in milk for 2-3 days, refrigerated. Stir or shake daily. Strain and serve hot or cold. Sip slowly.

You could also make a hot chocolate from this milk.

Olive Oil
Some patients may want to access their medicine through something other than the dessert course. Olive oil may be substituted for butter or canola oil in the crock pot process (Method II) and used, after careful straining, in any recipe calling for regular olive oil.

Line the inside of a strainer with two layers of cheesecloth, laid down perpendicular to each other. Pour the oil and leaf mixture into the strainer. Gather the cheesecloth from the bottommost layer and twist to extract additional oil. Squeeze until you are satisfied that the majority of the oil has been removed, and discard the cheesecloth and leaf.

I bought a focaccia bread mix at the grocery store, and used medicinal olive oil in the recipe, as well as combining with balsamic vinegar for dipping.

Dosage for the bread would be mild but would be increased greatly with direct oil and vinegar dipping. ✶

Now You're Cooking

Now it's time to turn your beautiful marijuana butter or oil into a favorite dessert or snack. We have leaned toward making cookies for patients for several reasons: they provide a consistent dose of medicine, they are easily stored and transported, they are readily available and can be used in social situations where "lighting up" the herb would draw unwanted attention to a patient, and the taste is familiar and desirable. Patients who have lost their appetite have reported that 1 cookie will stimulate their appetite and make it desirable to eat other much-needed foods.

Most standard cookie recipes call for sugar, flour and eggs, and samples are included here to use. Should the patient have dietary restrictions, look under Ingredient Substitutions on page 34 for recommended substitutions.

Any recipe that calls for butter or oil will work; simply follow the cookbook directions. I've searched through many cookbooks to find recipes that call for the highest butter content and have experimented with many combinations.

Here is a list of the recipes that follow:
• Basic Cookie Recipe
• Lemon Lace Cookies
• Quick Cannabis Chocolate
• Diet-Wise Coconut Banana Cookies
• Bliss Balls
• Honey Chocolates
• Honey Oatmeal Cookies
• Honey Whole Wheat Banana Bread
• Honey Pumpkin Bread
• Honey Chocolate Brownies
• Butterscotch Blondies
• Prepacked Mixes
• Marijuana Leaf Sugar Cookies
• Tinctures

Basic Cookie Recipe

Simply tasty, this easy-to-make cookie recipe is sure to be a hit. Optional ingredients let you add sweetness or make a chewier treat.

Ingredients:
- ³/₄ cup sugar
- 1 egg
- 1 cup marijuana butter
- 1 tablespoon vanilla or preferred extract for flavor
- 2¹/₂ cups flour
- 1 teaspoon baking soda
- ¹/₄ teaspoon salt

Preparation time: 30 minutes

Cooking time: Preheat oven to 350°F/177°C. Bake 4 at a time, 9–13 minutes per batch.

Yield: 4 dozen, each containing 1 teaspoon butter = medium dose

Instructions:
For basic dough, begin by mixing together until creamy:
- 1 cup marijuana butter
- ³/₄ cup sugar
- 1 egg
- 1 tablespoon vanilla or preferred extract for flavor

In a separate bowl, whisk or sift together:
- 2¹/₂ cups flour
- 1 teaspoon baking soda
- ¹/₄ teaspoon salt
- Optional spices you may add, according to personal taste: 1 teaspoon cinnamon, ginger, nutmeg, ground cloves or cardamom, lemon or lime zest, or other favorites

Stir flour mixture and spices into butter mixture.

Optional additions, which may be stirred in as desired to make a thicker, chewier cookie (note: reduce the amount of flour by ¹/₂ cup when adding

a cup of any of the following):
- up to 1 cup finely chopped walnuts, pecans or other nuts/seeds
- 1 cup oatmeal
- 1 cup toasted sesame seeds
- 1 cup chocolate chips (white or dark)
- 1 cup raisins or chopped dried fruit

The options you choose will alter the density of the batter. Roll into balls and flatten, or drop by the spoonful onto an ungreased cookie sheet. Try to be consistent with the size of each cookie. With practice, this will become automatic. This is the step that gives the patient the premeasured dose.

You may want to bake one cookie at this point to see if it bakes to the thickness you desire. If it's too thin, add more flour or other optional ingredients. If too thick, add 1–2 tablespoons of liquid—lemon or lime juice are nice additions.

Bake 9–13 minutes until cookies are browned around the edges.

To test the potency of the butter and recipe, eat ½ of a cookie and wait a couple of hours. Note the results. As mentioned earlier in the discussion of working out the correct proportions of herb to butter, this might be the time to start a journal and record the results, if you are new to this process. Be sure also to note the number of cookies you got from 1 cup of butter.

All of these cookies freeze well. Store them in sealed baggies or containers. ✳

Bliss's favorite

Lime/ Sesame Cookies
Using the previous basic cookie recipe, reduce flour to 2 cups and add 1 cup of toasted sesame seeds and the zest of two limes. If the batter is real stiff, add up to 3 tablespoons of lime juice. This makes a light and delicious cookie.

Lemon Lace Cookies

Silky smooth treats to sooth away your blues and bring you back to a brighter place.

Ingredients:
- 1 cup finely ground almonds*
- 1 cup sugar
- ¾ cup rolled oats
- ½ teaspoon salt
- ½ cup softened marijuana butter*
- 2 tablespoons vanilla
- 2 tablespoons lemon juice
- 1 tablespoon lemon zest
- 1 tablespoon water

*Substitutions:
- Ground pecans, walnuts or macadamia nuts can be substituted for the almonds.
- Marijuana coconut oil can be used instead of the marijuana butter. (No other oils work, however.)
- Up to 1 tablespoon of ground ginger can be added to make an extra-spicy cookie.

Preparation time: 30 minutes

Cooking time: Preheat oven 350°F/177°C. Bake 6 at a time, 6–8 minutes per batch.

Yield: 4 dozen = ½ teaspoon butter per cookie = mild dose

Instructions:
Mix dry ingredients together: ground almonds, sugar, rolled oats, flour, salt and ginger, if used. Cream in the butter, using the back of a large

spoon. Add the vanilla, lemon juice and lemon zest. If the dough is excessively dry, add up to 1 tablespoon water.

Use nonstick cookie sheets or line cookie sheets with parchment paper. Moisten hands and roll dough into small balls. If you use too much dough, they will spread out and merge into one big cookie! Flatten with the palm of your hand. These cookies may bake with a lump in the middle if left in a ball. Bake for 6–8 minutes, checking frequently, and remove from the oven when the edges begin to brown and the center is bubbling.

Allow to cool before removing from the parchment paper. These delicate cookies can be made more potent by dipping half of each cookie into melted Quick Cannabis Chocolate (on page 25). After dipping, hold the cookie over the pan to catch any dripping chocolate and then place on a cooling rack or a clean sheet of parchment paper to set.

These cookies come out very thin and crispy, like candied lace. They don't travel well but are a very popular cookie, especially with patients who have experienced a loss of appetite but still have a sweet tooth. ✳

Quick Cannabis Chocolate

A devilishly sweet treat that is sure to delight and help the healing process.

Ingredients:
- 4 ounces* of a favorite chocolate bar or chips of chocolate
- 2 tablespoons* of soft cannabis butter or cannabis coconut oil

*Note: This can be made in larger batches, too, keeping this same ratio of chocolate to butter/oil.

Preparation time: 15 minutes

Yield: If cut or molded into 1 dozen pieces, each will contain ½ teaspoon of butter/oil = mild dose

Instructions:

This quick chocolate treat is made by simply melting your favorite chocolate (presweetened chocolate

chips, or bars of sweet chocolate), stirring in the marijuana butter or coconut oil, and remolding.

In a double boiler, or a stainless steel bowl placed over a sauce pan, slowly melt the chocolate over boiling water, stirring continuously with a rubber spatula. Add the butter and stir until completely incorporated.

Remove from heat. Stir for a minute or two as the chocolate cools. Pour on a piece of parchment paper or a nonstick cookie sheet, or into chocolate molds.

To remove chocolate from the molds, allow to cool, or put in the freezer for up to 3 minutes. Invert on a flat surface and tap to release chocolate from the mold.

Chocolate molds can be purchased in fine kitchen stores and should come with directions for using. I like using molds because each piece has a consistent amount of butter and is easy to use as a single dose. The chocolate really does help make the medicine go down! ✱

Diet-Wise Coconut Banana Cookies

If you want a healthy treat with an intense flavor burst, this cookies the one for you.

Ingredients:
- 1 cup pitted dates
- 2 cups of rolled oats
- ½ cup cannabis coconut oil, softened
- 1 tablespoon vanilla
- 1 cup shredded coconut
- ½ teaspoon salt
- ripe bananas

Optional:
- 1 tablespoon of cinnamon for added flavor
- Coatings of coconut, sesame seeds or ground nuts

Preparation time: 20 minutes

Cooking time: Preheat oven to 350°F/177°C. Bake each sheet of 12 cookies for 12–15 minutes per batch.

Yield: 2 dozen = 1 teaspoon oil per cookie = medium dose

Instructions:

Put ingredients, one at a time, into a food processor, pulsing to incorporate, in the order listed: dates, oats, oil, vanilla, coconut, salt, and ripe bananas. Pulse until a dough is formed.

These can be dropped by heaping teaspoons onto an ungreased cookie sheet. For a smoother cookie, roll into balls. Dampen your hands first with a small amount of water to prevent sticking.

Roll balls in small bowls of the following coatings—coconut, sesame seeds, finely chopped nuts—or leave plain. Place on ungreased cookies sheets and flatten with the palm of your hand.

For a really fancy treat, make a thumbprint in the center of each cookie and fill it with a scoop of your favorite jelly or jam. Bake for 12–15 minutes, removing when the cookies just begin to brown. ✸

Bliss Balls

This savory treat is ideal if you prefer to avoid sugar or flour. Bliss Balls can also be made with coconut oil for bite-sized snacks that are "dairy-free."

Ingredients:
- 1 cup of marijuana butter
- 2 cups of chopped nuts
- 1 or 2 cups of seeds
- $\frac{1}{2}$ to 1 cup of dates
- 1 cup of shredded coconut
- 1 cup other dried fruit

Optional: carob powder

Preparation time: 1 hour

Yield: 4 dozen, each containing 1 teaspoon butter = medium dose

Instructions:

This is an uncooked nut/seed ball that needs to be refrigerated in order for it to keep its form. There is no sugar or flour in this recipe, so it is ideal for people with restricted diets. The coconut oil produced in method IV was developed for this recipe, for folks on a dairy-free diet. You can use either of the butters. The method II oil will not work because it doesn't harden when cooled.

This is a very flexible recipe. Choose your favorite nuts and seeds in any combination. Sometimes I finely chop everything and the "dough" is much like a flour dough. Other times I put large pieces of nuts and seeds in for a really chewy treat. Experiment to find what pleases your palate best.

Gently melt the coconut oil or butter in a pan of warm water until it becomes liquid.

Note the white color of the coconut oil in the picture (top of next page). Once the oil is melted, it returns to a beautiful green color.

Melting the butter

Measure the butter

Add to ingredients

Add carob powder

Add smoothie

Measure 1 cup of butter. Measuring the amount of marijuana butter or coconut oil is critical if you need to have measured doses. Set aside.

In a large bowl, mix together the following. Hands work best for this:

- 2 cups chopped nuts (any combination of raw almonds, pecans, hazelnuts, cashews, macadamia nuts or others will work) These can be chopped in a food processor or by hand.
- 1–2 cups of seeds (any combination of sesame, sunflower, pumpkin or others) Lightly chop if desired or leave whole.
- ½–1 cup dates, chopped by hand or in food processor, according to need for sweetness
- 1 cup shredded coconut
- 1 cup other dried fruit. (raisins, craisins, apricots, mango, pineapple, or other favorites) Chop to size of seeds.
- carob powder (optional)

Add melted butter or oil, slowly pouring over nut/seed/fruit mixture and mixing with hands.

Add 1 tablespoon carob powder. Carob adds a chocolate-like flavor. This ingredient is optional. If you choose to leave it out, use less of the smoothie liquid in the next step or add more of the finely chopped dry ingredients from the list above to the mix to make up for this dry ingredient.

Make a smoothie in a blender with 1 cup of fruit juice (apple works well, but you can try others), a banana or other soft fruit, and chopped ginger if desired. Be creative. This adds to the flavor and sweetness of the finished product. Slowly pour this smoothie over mix, mixing in with your hands as you go. The amount you use will be by the "feel." Keep adding until the mix can be easily rolled into balls.

Roll mix into balls. Be sure to be consistent with the size of each ball.

The balls will be soft at this point, but will firm up when refrigerated.

Put finely chopped ingredients in small bowls to use as a coating. Roll each ball in a coating. Place on a cookie sheet and refrigerate until hardened. These need to be kept refrigerated because they fall apart easily at room temperature. To store Bliss Balls for more than a week, we recommend freezing in baggies or an airtight container to avoid the freezer taste. ✶

A Word About Ingredient Substitutions

Many patients have food allergies or sensitivities that make it necessary to adapt recipes to meet those needs. For example, one patient for whom I bake cannot tolerate refined sugar. I've found it easy, with experience and over several trial batches, to adjust the recipes to allow for more liquid (in the case of substituting honey for granulated sugar) and to include ingredients like fruit or nuts that either add or absorb moisture, respectively. If your batter is too wet, add a small amount of flour and mix well until the batter reaches a doughy consistency. If your batter is too dry, add water, an egg, or a liqueur (for more flavor). There are infinite possibilities; just experiment, keeping in mind the needs of those for whom you are baking. It's always good to ask patients if they have any food sensitivities when you first discuss baking for them.

Many patients have allergies to flour or wheat products. There are lots of ways to substitute for wheat flour, but keep in mind that each kind of flour will translate into a different sort of flavor in the finished cookie. Spelt flour is one substitution that works for some patients and tastes the most like wheat flour. Substituting rice flour will change the taste of your cookie; you'll want to choose a recipe like an almond crescent cookie that is more compatible with the flavor of rice flour than recipes that are traditionally European. You may also find wheatless mixes at your local health food store.

Here is the recipe I use for patients who cannot tolerate refined sugar. It is an old recipe that originally included brown sugar. I simply used more honey rather than substituting another kind of sweetener in adapting this.

If you have trouble finding alternative ingredients, ask at a natural foods store, or contact The Baker's Catalogue, P.O. Box 876, Norwich, Vermont 05055-0876. 1-800-827-6836. www.bakerscatalogue.com ✳

Honey Chocolates

For a fast acting medicine and that appeals to your sweet tooth, try this incredible sugar-free treat.

Ingredients:
For a recipe without refined sugar:
- 1½ lbs. Unsweetened chocolate
- 3 cups honey
- 1½ cups cannabis butter
- Ground or chopped nuts (optional)

For a recipe with some refined sugar:
- 1½ lbs. Semi-sweet chocolate
- 1 cup honey
- 1½ cups cannabis butter
- Ground or chopped nuts (optional)

Tools:
- Crock-pot
- Wooden spoon
- Digital or candy thermometer
- 14"x18" baking sheet with one inch sides
- Parchment paper

Instructions:
Using high quality chocolate and the wonder appliance known as the crock-pot, you can make potent medicine that is a bit quicker acting than other edibles.

Place the chocolate, cannabis butter and honey in the crock-pot and heat on low. Stir repeatedly, every few minutes. About the time all the ingredients are melted, you should put the thermometer in the liquid. When the temperature reaches 100°F, stir even more often, carefully avoiding the thermometer. When the mixture reaches 130°F, turn the crock-pot off. Continue to stir the chocolate until it cools down to 80 degrees F or less. This is called "tempering" the chocolate and helps it to stay more solid. The more slowly this process goes the better. When the chocolate is cooler than 80 degrees F, pour it into a baking sheet with one inch sides lined with parchment paper. [Optional: Sprinkle the top with hazelnut meal or any ground or chopped nuts.] Let the mixture sit and cool for at least an hour, and then carefully put it in the refrigerator. Several hours later, you can pick up the cooled chocolate by the parchment paper, and slide it onto a cutting board. Cut the chocolate into 1-inch squares.

The Dosage is high, due to a high butter to ingredient ratio. Keep the chocolates refrigerated at all times. ✱

Honey Oatmeal Cookies

If you are avoiding sugar but still crave a sweet treat, these chewy cookies will hit the spot.

Ingredients:
- 1 cup marijuana butter (at room temperature)
- 2½ cups honey
- 5 eggs
- 2½ cups flour
- 2 teaspoons salt
- 1¼ teaspoons baking soda
- 7½ cups quick oats
- 1 cup of any of the following ingredients: chopped dates, figs, apples, carrots, raisins, currants, chocolate chips, nuts and seeds

Preparation time: 30 minutes

Cooking time: Preheat oven to 350°F/177°C. Bake 5 at a time, 10–12 minutes per batch.

Yield: 5 dozen cookies, each with less than 1 teaspoon butter = medium dose.

Instructions:
Spray baking sheets with nonstick spray.

Blend the marijuana butter, honey and egg thoroughly.

Add flour, salt and baking soda and mix well.

Add the quick oats and any of the fruit or nuts in any combination. This allows for more variety within this one recipe.

Drop by heaping tablespoons onto greased cookie sheets. Bake for 10–12 minutes. Let cool for 3–5 minutes on baking sheets, then transfer to a cooling rack.

Note: This cookie dough freezes very well. One of my patients lives quite a distance away, and I can get much more medicine to her at one time by giving her dough that her husband defrosts and bakes at a later time, thereby having fresh, instead of frozen cookies. ✹

Honey Whole Wheat Banana Bread

Another wholesome treat, that will tantalize your palate and soothe your pains without sacrificing flavor.

Ingredients:
• 1 cup marijuana butter or oil
• 1½ cups honey
• 2 eggs
• 2 cups whole wheat flour
• 1 cup unbleached white flour
• 2 teaspoons baking soda
• 1 teaspoon sea salt
• 4 bananas, mashed

Preparation time: 30 minutes

Cooking Time: Preheat oven to 350°F/177°C. Bake for 45 minutes.

Yield: 8 small loaves, each cut into 12 pieces, each with 1 teaspoon of butter = medium potency.

Instructions:
Grease 2 large or 3 medium loaf pans.

Mix mashed bananas, honey, room temperature butter or oil, and egg well.

Add dry ingredients (flours, soda and salt). Stir just enough to combine thoroughly.

Spoon into greased baking pans. Bake 50 or 60 minutes, or until a toothpick removes clean, or the bread springs back when you touch it. Overbaking will cause quick breads to become crumbly. Let sit in the pan for at least 10 minutes, then turn onto a rack to cool. ✦

Honey Pumpkin Bread

Not just a seasonal treat, this bread will delight your taste buds and keep you in high spirits all year round.

Ingredients:
- 2¹/₂ cups honey
- 1 cup marijuana butter or oil
- 3 cups pumpkin puree*
- 2 cups chopped dates
- 2 cups chopped walnuts
- 2 teaspoons sea salt
- 2 teaspoons cinnamon
- 2 teaspoons ground cloves
- 2 teaspoons baking soda
- 4 cups unbleached white flour
- 5 cups whole wheat flour
- 1 cup wheat germ

Instructions:
Preheat oven to 350°F. Grease 4 large or 5–6 medium loaf pans.

Mix the honey, room temperature butter or oil, pumpkin, dates, walnuts, salt, cinnamon, cloves and baking soda in a large mixing bowl. Mix thoroughly. Stir in the remaining ingredients (flours and wheat germ).

Spoon into the greased loaf pans.

Bake for 1 hour or until done. Cool in the pans for at least 20 minutes, and then turn onto a cooling rack.

*I use Halloween pumpkins that I cut up, skin, cook and mash the day after Halloween night. I make sure not to carve them until just before dark, and take them inside when the trick-or-treaters stop coming. I store the pumpkins in the refrigerator until I can process them, and the mashed pumpkin freezes very well. ✳

Honey Chocolate Brownies

Here is another recipe adapted to an all-honey version.

Ingredients:
- 1 cup melted marijuana butter or oil
- ½ cup melted unsweetened chocolate or cocoa powder
- 4 eggs
- 1 cup honey
- 2 teaspoons vanilla
- 2 cups unbleached white flour
- 2 teaspoons baking powder
- ½ teaspoon sea salt
- 1 cup raisins
- 1 cup chopped nuts

Preparation Time: 30 minutes

Cooking Time: Preheat the oven to 350°F/177°C. Bake for 45 minutes.

Yield: Using a 9" x 13" pan, cut into 24 equal pieces (approximately 2" x 2"), each serving has 2 teaspoons of butter = high dose, or cut into 48 pieces (about 2" x 1") = medium dose.

Instructions:
Whip the butter, chocolate, carob or cocoa, and honey together until smooth. Add eggs and vanilla, mix well.

Add the dry ingredients, stir until dampened. Add the raisins and nuts and mix thoroughly.

Pour batter into a greased 9 x 13-inch baking pan. Bake for 45 minutes or until done. ✳

Butterscotch Blondies

Many people love blondes and this sweet treat is one that everyone is sure to love. Either cut them large for a little extra kick or cut them small for a more medium dose.

Ingredients:
- 1 cup marijuana butter
- 4 cups brown sugar
- 4 eggs
- 1 teaspoon vanilla
- 2 cups unbleached white flour
- 1 teaspoon baking powder
- 2 teaspoons sea salt
- 2 cups chopped mixed nuts (unsalted)

Preparation Time: 30 minutes

Cooking Time: Preheat the oven to 350°F/177°C. Bake for 45 minutes.

Yield: Using a 13" x 24" pan, cut into 24 equal pieces (approximately 4" x 3"), each serving has 2 teaspoons of butter = high dose, or cut into 48 pieces (about 2" x 3") = medium dose.

Instructions:
This recipe is full of sugar—brown sugar, that is. It takes well to spelt flour or other alternatives to wheat flour. Be sure to experiment with a bit of your dough, and taste to make sure the flour alternative does not adversely affect the flavor of your recipe.

Melt the marijuana butter in a large saucepan. Add the brown sugar, and stir until gloppy. Take off the heat immediately.

Place the saucepan on a hot pad and allow the mixture to cool slightly. Add the eggs slowly, making sure that the heat of the mixture does not coagulate the egg. Add the vanilla and mix thoroughly.

Add the flour, baking powder and salt and mix well. Stir in the chopped mixed nuts.

Pour into a greased 13 x 24-inch baking pan. Bake 45 minutes or until done. Do not overbake! ✳

Prepacked Mixes

Here's the big secret: if you don't have any special dietary needs and don't have to watch calories (or don't care to), you can use these butters in any store-bought mix that calls for butter or oil. The dosage that you get from each kind of cookie, cake or quick bread mix depends on the ratio of butter to the rest of the ingredients in the recipe. A cookie recipe with more butter in it (or butter called for on the package) is going to have a stronger dosage. A chocolate chip, sugar or butter cookie mix will probably have a stronger effect than an oatmeal or oatmeal chocolate chip cookie recipe mix, because of the fact that the oatmeal is an additional ingredient that disperses the butter more widely within the batch.

Follow the instructions on the mix package, and replace the butter or oil it calls for with the marijuana butter or oil. Add all the rest of the ingredients called for in the mix, and bake as directed. Remember what's already been said about adding nuts or fruits or liquids to keep the dough or batter at the right consistency—not too runny, not too dry.

My favorite way to spice up a store-bought brownie mix is to add spiced brandy (Korbel Extra Smooth) instead of the water called for in the recipe. The alcohol evaporates in the baking process, and all that's left is flavor! Experiment and be creative about adding different spices, fruits, nuts, seeds, and dried fruits to different mixes and enjoy the results.

You can make a delicious brownie cookie from a packaged brownie mix as well. Add more flour (about a cup, to make the brownie batter into a stiffer cookie dough) and include ¼ cup Kahlua, brandy or any liqueur with water called for in the recipe, eggs as called for, and 1 teaspoon of cinnamon. Mix into a stiff dough, drop by heaping teaspoonful onto a cookie sheet and bake 10 minutes at 350°. ✹

Here is how I prepare a mix:

Pour the mix into the bowl.

Add the marijuana butter and other ingredients as directed on the package.

Mix and bake as directed on the package. Enjoy!

Marijuana Leaf Sugar Cookies

These tasty treats can be made in a snap. Add your own extra touches to spice them up.

One thing the prepackaged mixes allow for is more time to be creative! These extra touches can be especially important for patients who don't have much appetite or may be very emotionally reliant on their medicine. Showing a little creativity, expending extra time and effort, or just placing a little love and healing intentionally into your work certainly can't hurt the healing or pain management process.

Here's how I make the Marijuana Leaf Sugar Cookies from a prepackaged sugar cookie mix. You can get a cannabis cookie cutter by calling (541) 338-9720 or on the Internet at www.houseofwah.com.

Mix the dough as directed on the package, and chill as directed. This is important to the rolling process. With the chilled dough, make balls that are about 6 inches in diameter. Prepare your

rolling surface by cleaning it thoroughly and dusting with white flour. Place the ball of dough on the surface.

Roll out the dough to a consistent ¼-inch thickness.

Dip the cookie cutter in flour and press into the rolled dough. You could also spray the cookie cutter with cooking spray before you start using it as well. You would only have to spray it once, whereas you will dip the cookie cutter in the flour each time you press it into the dough. Repeat pressing the cookie cutter into the dough until you have filled the rolled dough with cut cookies.

Carefully, gently remove the extra dough from around the cut cookies. Use a spatula to carefully remove the cut cookies from the rolling surface and place them on the cookie sheet.

Before baking, sprinkle the cookies on the cookie sheet with cinnamon sugar.

Bake as directed on the package. When the cookies are done, let cool on the cookie sheet for at least 10 minutes, then carefully use the spatula to remove each cookie

Carefully arrange the cookies on a plate because after all, presentation *is* everything!

Enjoy! ✶

Tinctures

A strong punch that can be used to deliver medicine quickly, but be careful about measuring your dosage.

Ingredients:
- 1 pint vodka, brandy or any hard liquor
- 2 oz. Cannabis leaf

Materials:
- 1 pint mason jar and lid
- Blender
- Strainer
- Cheesecloth
- Small blue or brown glass bottles with droppers (these are sold in many natural foods stores)
- A small funnel

Instructions:
A tincture is an extract of a resin or essence by combining with alcohol. Once extracted and with the leaf removed, the resultant liquid can be taken directly under the tongue or mixed with water or juice. Any natural foods store has a plethora of herbal tinctures to use for many purposes. Medical cannabis patients or caregivers can make tinctures themselves very easily.

Cold extraction:
One way to make a speedy tincture in three to four days is by using the freezer. Put the leaf in the 1 pint mason jar, cover with vodka (or any other liquor). Put the jar in a paper bag, and then

Cold process

Dark place process

place the jar (in the paper bag) in your freezer. Shake the jar at least once a day. After three to four days, remove from the freezer. Process as below and put the liquid into the bottles.

Dark place extraction

For this method, I used a spiced brandy as the alcohol base. Place the leaf in the pint mason jar. Cover with the brandy. Close the jar snugly and place it in a brown paper bag. Place in a cupboard or other cool, dark place. Shake daily for 3–4 weeks. The concoction can actually sit for up to six months with regular shaking. After the desired sitting time, remove from the dark place.

Removing the leaf material:

Line a strainer with cheesecloth, placing it crosswise inside the strainer. Place the strainer over a large bowl, preferably with a spout for pouring. Pour the leaf and alcohol mixture into the lined strainer. Pull the cheesecloth up around the leaf by the bottommost layer of the cheesecloth, and twist the ends of the cloth together in order to squeeze the alcohol out of the leaf

Discard the leaf. Some sources say that you can use the leftover cheesecloth for burns or skin irritations, but I'm not clear on how you might store the unrinsed cheesecloth until it is needed. Using the small funnel, pour the tincture into the dropper bottles. You can cut down a coffee filter and line the funnel, or use a small strainer or half of a tea ball, as I did. Be sure to store the bottles in a cool, dark place.

Dosage: High when taken directly, Moderately high when diluted in water. Depending on the potency of leaf used, 5–15 drops per dose. ✹

Afterword: Visiting a Cannabis Doctor

Veronica Greene

I had injured my back at work and was creating a relationship with workman's compensation when I heard about "Dr. Sam" (his name has been changed). He was not attached to an HMO or any other kind of insurance, and I would have to pay him in cash. After speaking to his office staff, I found that I needed to submit all my medical records to him. I gathered all the records from my HMO and the rapidly growing collection from workman's comp and presented them to Dr. Sam for review. About a week later his office called, and I was accepted for an appointment.

My first consultation was an hour long, at a cost of $200.00. What a luxury, to spend an hour with a doctor just talking about myself and my medical issues, and what has been done thus far to control pain and inflammation. I have a delicate stomach and have been identified with irritable bowel syndrome, and I cannot take most traditional painkillers and anti-inflammatories (I do take one Naprosin per day). For this reason, combined with osteoarthritis and degenerative disc disease, I was deemed eligible for approval for receiving medical marijuana. My approval would last for six months, after which I would have to return for a follow-up appointment. Dr. Sam made one stipulation to my approval: I would need to consistently lose weight over time in order to keep my approval valid. I was identified with diabetes at the time and was considerably overweight.

I have now been seeing Dr. Sam for three years, and each visit is a joy. He has seen me through a hysterectomy, and more symptoms of the osteoarthritis. Each time he gently and consistently urges for vaporized ingestion because it is the least harmful to the lungs (and least dangerous to the hips). He will see me yearly from now on, because he can consistently chart a weight loss, over the last three years, of forty pounds. I feel so lucky to have the approval and to be able to access a second medical opinion from someone who knows me and who isn't required to "diagnose by formula," as so many HMO doctors are required to do.

Afterword: Visiting a Cannabis Dispensary

Bliss Cameron

Once Proposition 215 was passed in California, patients who had the approval or recommendation of a physician to use marijuana were permitted medical use, but the question of access had not been clearly addressed. I wasn't able to grow my own medicine, so I was dependent on other sources. At that time there were no dispensaries in my own county, so I called a dispensary in a different county and was told that I could sign up with them if I brought a letter from my doctor and a photo ID card. I needed to make an appointment to discuss my needs with a nurse who had been hired by this club to do intake for new members.

When the day arrived I was nervous, knowing that visiting a dispensary was a legal risk. No patients had been prosecuted, but I was still apprehensive. This club was located in a small community theater just off a main road. I had a friend come with me, but she had to stay in the car because she wasn't a recognized patient. The first things I noticed when I walked in were surveillance cameras and monitors behind the reception desk. But a volunteer greeted

me warmly and I began to relax.

I was ushered to the back to meet with the nurse and had an uplifting conversation, as I shared my medical history, my letter of approval from a major HMO, and my experiences with marijuana as a medicine. As I look back, this was an experience that helped me understand how important marijuana was for me. The mental shift from being a "law breaker" to being a legitimate patient was incredible! After this interview, I was accepted as a member of this "club" and a picture ID card was made. I was assured that all records were confidential and secured for the safety of the patients.

It was time to make a purchase. There was a display counter with pipes, rolling papers and baked goods to buy, and a menu of six different strains of marijuana at prices from $25 to $50 for an eighth of an ounce, or $150 to $350 an ounce. Prices were as high as on the street, but the source and quality were assured and I realized there was a large overhead to run this club. After making the purchase, I decided to "medicate"

To find out more about the current status and location of dispensaries you can go to the following Web sites:

Americans for Safe Access:
safeaccessnow.org

California NORML:
canorml.org

www.marijuana-uses.com

www.lindesmith.org

www.mpp.org

www.norml.org

www.wamm.org

ARTHRITIS

Tom, a rheumatoid arthritis patient for 11 years, has severe form of this illness

"Prescription medication was ineffective at arresting my symptoms. Moments after use, cannabis relieves me of the physical and mental pain."

Americans for Medical Relief

before leaving, as this club encouraged socialization with other patients. The theater provided a comfortable environment. This social aspect of clubs has come into question, being restricted in some areas. I found this to be one of the real advantages of going to a club.

There are now over 150 recognized dispensaries in the state, allowed to operate or tolerated by local government officials. I applaud the courage and conviction of the individuals running these clubs, at personal risk, to provide both a source of medicine and a social environment for patients. ✶

Index